God's DIVINE ORDER IN Marriage . . .

God's
DIVINE ORDER IN
Marriage . . .
REVEALING GOD'S HEART.

Dr Beatrice Hornsby

Library of Congress Control Number: 2017908850
ISBN: Hardcover   978-1-5434-2848-3
                  Softcover   978-1-5434-2847-6
                  eBook   978-1-5434-2846-9

Print information available on the last page.

Rev. date: 06/05/2017

To order additional copies of this book, contact:
Xlibris
1-888-795-4274
www.Xlibris.com
Orders@Xlibris.com
762048

I dedicate this book to my Lord and savior Jesus Christ, to my wonderful husband and children who stood by me daily and who the Lord used to teach me so much.

To my dear big brother James Agorsor who was used by the Lord to encourage and sponsor this work.

I bless God for all of you.

Hebrews 11:4a Amp.

> "Let marriage be held in honor (esteemed worthy, precious of great price and especially dear) in all things."

Foreword

In today's world, the institution of marriage has suffered much at the hands of humanity. Our world has changed and evolved so much that one cannot just define what marriage is without raising so much controversy.

It is a blessing to know that God, the sovereign one, the creator of all things instituted marriage. He was not confused when he set up the institution of marriage; neither should we be confused as to what marriage is and what it is not. His word, being the very manual for living his kind of life distinctly defines to us what marriage is and how he expects us to perceive and practice that art. Only through the word of God can we perceive and understand the concept of marriage.

The enemy our adversary is out to destroy the institution of marriage by causing perverse and debased minds to interpret and say what it is and what it is not.

Marriage was instituted in the Garden of Eden. God established this blessed union between male and female. It was not supposed to be a contract it was supposed to be a covenant, an ever binding covenant never to be broken, God being part of it. It is supposed to be held as a sacred, divine covenant between a man and woman and God.

Why are our marriages facing problems both in the circular world and the Christian world? What has gone wrong in our world, how is it so hard to find long lasting marriages now. I beg to differ but may submit to all, that we have departed from following the very blue print of this institution; from going to its creator and originator to ask about how to make it work.

Brothers and Sisters, like the manual given by the manufacturers of a car to the buyer so he or she would know how every part of it operates, So should we go to our manual (the Bible) on marriage given to us by its originator and designer God, so we can portray from his perspective how it ought to be. In so doing we will reap the benefits of such a great institution.

I submit to you not so much in enticing words but simply with a stuttering tongue my heart cry for what I believe we ought to see in our marriages today. Yes great men and women have written volumes about this, but as a simple daughter of my father may I with his help let all who read this hear His passion and heart cry as to what we ought to do, see, and how we ought to live in our marriages.

My prayer is that in some way what I write and share will cause the reader to want more of God in their marriage and seek to build their marriages according to God's pattern.

CHAPTER ONE

Gods System

We must realize that God is a God of systems, principles, patterns and order. He puts systems in place to create order and these systems are interdependent. In Genesis we see order in God's creation; in the building of the Moses Tabernacle we see distinct order and detailing.

The first chapter of the book of Ecclesiastes 1:5-7 (Amp Version) makes us see this clearly, "The Sun also rises and the sun goes down, and hastens to the place where it arose, the wind goes toward the south, and turns around to the North. The wind whirls about continually and comes again on the circuit. All the rivers run into the sea; yet the sea is not full".

God's set systems are governed by principles; the systems can work effectively and be in alignment with His expectations only when they are built upon His principles. This can be seen in the creation account in the book of Genesis, in family life and in the church as an organism and an institution.

In God's system, he establishes rules or shall we say a government with chains of command. There is always a head to whom people are responsible to and who is accountable to the people he governs. In the institution of marriage for example, the husband is the head, in the church it is the Pastor or under shepherd to the flock, in the corporate world and market place it is the Chief Executive or Managing Director.

The God we serve is truly the only wise God, for in his inspired book the Bible, he has indeed given us the blueprint to living peaceably in this world system though as his children we do not belong to the world but live in it. (John 17:16)

Another ingredient which makes God's system work effectively is when there is agreement or unity as his children effect principles. The book (Amos 3:3 Amp Version) plainly expresses this. "Do two walk together except they make an appointment and have agreed?"

Having the above as a background, since our issue is to determine what the divine order in marriage is, I will define what "marriage" is, from God's perspective since He alone is the originator of such an institution.

The definition of marriage has been distorted and changed with society evolving day by day, but from our Judeo Christian point of view, we can say that Marriage as instituted by God is "to co-join, to enter into a close union, to unite, to fuse, to couple, a connection between a man and woman". Romans 8:17 will help us see marriage from the perspective of the Church and Christ as being two people participating as one and having a common goal and interest being common participants just as God's children are conjoined and heirs with Christ. Romans 8:17(Amp) reads "And if we are His children then we are his Heirs also: heirs of God and fellow heirs with Christ ". (sharing His inheritance with Him).

CHAPTER TWO

The Mind Of God Concerning Marriage

The book of (Hebrew 13:4 Amp Version) explicitly tells us how God sees marriage and how he wants us to see it. "Let marriage be held in honor (esteemed worthy, precious, of great price, and especially dear in all things).

Honor means to show respect, to bring pride and pleasure. Marriage being honorable means it is something that brings pride, pleasure and esteem to those involved in it. This is God's intent. Here we must see how God views marriage and see that he has already honored marriage, ours is to keep it that way, with his help because it is his institution.

Once God is the institutor of marriage, we must know from his perspective how he wants us to keep it running, and also know how he expects the marriage covenant to function.

In Genesis 1:26-28 (amp version) We read, "And God said, Let us (Father, Son and Holy Spirit) make mankind in our image, after our likeness, and let them have complete authority over the fish of the sea, the birds of the air, the (tame) beasts, and over all of the earth, and over everything that creeps upon the earth

Verse 27: So God created man in His own image, in the image and likeness of God, He created him : male and female He created them.

Verse 28: And God blessed them and said to them, be fruitful, multiply, and fill the earth, and subdue it (using all its vast resources in the service of God and man); and have dominion over the fish of the sea, the birds of the air, and over every living creature that moves upon the earth

We can see here that when it came to creation the three persons of God were involved. This paints a picture for us to see God's mind pertaining to the workings of our marriage; for God always does things in "threes", the Father, Son and Holy Spirit are always involved in whatever he does. God's intent is to be involved in the institution of marriage.

He said in (Verse 26) "Let us make man in our own image and likeness". This immediately brings to mind a form, an order of doing things. It tells us that where there is no image there is no likeness, there definitely will be no order. This in relation to marriage is to help us to know that when marriage is not resembling what God ordained it to be, where the whole trinity will be involved in, where the parties in the marriage do not conform to the likeness and image of the creator, there will definitely be no dominion, fruitfulness or a replenishing.

The image of God is the true being of God, His image is His faculty, and abilities referred to as "Suban" in Hebrew. God's character is his righteousness; and he manifested this nature in relation with Adam and Eve in the garden; he made them like himself and in the cool of the day he would come to have fellowship with them.

We can deduce from here that only when couples in marriage establish righteousness in their marriages, where they make this nature of God that he has given to them to be the character and nature of their marriages, will they see the fullness of God's divine order. Couples can exercise their divine character of righteousness in their marriages, only when they decide to walk in constant fellowship with God whose likeness they are. It is only then that couples can exercise their dominion over the attacks of the enemy in their marriages. Note that God made man righteous (to be as He is), then commanded them to be one, then He made them fruitful; and asked them to replenish the earth.

In Genesis 3:8-11, The devil sought to bring disorder in God's ordained system; he sought to cut off Adam and Eve's foundation in marriage by luring them to step out of their nature of righteousness, a right standing with God by causing them to sin. We can say therefore that marriage is important because the destruction of its foundation which is righteousness affects everyone or everything about it.

Chaos and disorder in marriage is caused by both or either parties not effecting or walking in their righteousness. This is not about doing righteousness but according to Romans 6:18 "You have become the servants of righteousness of conformity to the divine will in thought, purpose and actions. It is either the husband is not walking in his God ordained role as submitting totally to God and then loving the wife as Christ loves HIS church, and the wife is also not submitting to the husband as unto the Lord and not submitting totally to the Lord as well.

Couples not being spiritually motivated but fleshly motivated in their marriage will not please God. In Genesis 3:6, Eve saw the tree was pleasant and suitable and that it was good for food, was delightful to look at, and a tree to be desired in order to make one wise, she took of its fruit and ate and gave some also to her husband and he ate. We can see here the lust of the eyes, lust of the flesh and the pride of life being manifested here in the life of the first couple.

Having a right standing with God, acknowledging your fellowship and righteousness with him allows one to be able to relate with him, and walk according to his purpose in marriage. Chaos breaks down divine order, and Lucifer broke divine order in heaven and caused chaos. Couples choosing to live outside God's divine order will automatically reap discord in their marriages.

In Genesis 6:1-6 we see that pursuant of God's desire for one in marriage, pertaining to choices made will yield godly results. Deciding to go one's own way and neglecting God's desire leads to chaos, sin and strive.

CHAPTER THREE

Repairing The Broken System

We read from Genesis chapter one the beautiful story of creation and how God had a well laid out system of order even in nature. In the twenty seventh verse of the same chapter, God created man in his own image and likeness male and female. Genesis 2:7 is the very picture of how God formed man from the dust of the ground and breathed into his nostrils the breath or spirit of life, and man became a living being.

God had to breath into man His Righteousness his life force, His Spirit, and man became a living soul. This breath of God that man received from his creator God, made man able to relate to God through and with his spirit.

We know as the story unfolds in Genesis that Adam and Eve disobeyed God and as a result, they spiritually died to the consciousness of God. They were spiritually dead, unto God but physically alive. This is what humankind inherited from the first parents. Sin entered the world, fellowship with God became strained, Adam and Eve were banished by God from the Gardens of Eden, and lost the intimate fellowship they had with God their creator.

Adam and Eve committed treason against God as they sided with the devil to disobey their creator. Humankind inherited a sinful nature from their parents and that became the adamic sin nature of man. As a parent, I can imagine the pain in God's heart seeing his beloved children turn against him to have their own way not his perfect way. In his mercy, he had to reconcile man back to him for order to be restored between He God the creator and his creation.

God reconciled man back to him by sending the second Adam Yeshuah the anointed One (Jesus Christ) to give up his blood by sacrificing his life for humankind. We must note here that according to Genesis 2:7 the first Adam became a living soul but he quickened the spirit of man through Yeshuah's sacrifice for man to be reconciled to God to restore the order that was broken in the garden of Eden according to 1 Corinthians 15:45, the second Adam being Jesus.

Now let me explain here that Adam is called the first Adam, because he is the root as it were from which we spring. And Christ is the latter man, because he is the beginning of all those that are spiritual, and in him we are all included. Christ is called a spirit, by reason of that most excellent nature, that is to say God who dwells in him bodily, as Adam is called a living soul by reason of the soul which is the best part in him.

We can deduce and infer from the above scriptures that as pertains to God's divine order to be upheld in our marriages, we must be reconciled to God by having a personal relationship with Him. There is no way we as God's creation can have and experience God's best for us in our marriages. Our spirit must be alive unto God, quickened by Jesus Christ through His Spirit of truth, The Holy Spirit. We must make a note of this fact that God presented Eve to Adam after He God had breathed into Him his breath of life. There can be no living active presence of the Lord in your marriage if you have not received the quickening of the Lord.

As God gave His life to the first man's soul through breathing into Him, He God's own breath (life), Adam could hear and communicate with his creator God.

If we are not alive unto God spiritually as his creation through our spirits being quickened by salvation unto him, there is absolutely no way we can hear from Him to be able to know what He God desires in our marriages. We may try in our own human way with our own human wisdom, use customs and traditions of man to make our marriages work. This will definitely not meet the standard of our creator, for he alone has the blueprint for marriage, and besides nothing done from the fleshly perspective will ever meet his standards, that which is generated out from a regenerated life giving spirit pleases him. All believers must ask the Lord to guide them to their God ordained spouses. Men and women cannot choose their spouses based on the natural endowments such as looks, wealth, nor anything physical motivated by the carnal mind. The book of Proverbs 31:30(Amp) says charm and grace are deceptive, and beauty is vain (because it is not lasting) but a woman who reverently fears the Lord she shall be praised. Also in the tenth verse of the same chapter, we read "who can find a virtuous woman?, for her price is far above rubies". We can deduce from this scripture that only our God by the holy spirit can help anyone to discern and choose the man or woman divinely assigned and appointed for them.

God brought his life once again into man through Jesus Christ as he made man righteous, justifying, sanctifying and redeeming man, man's sprit is quickened. This goes to suggest that the marriage life should have the spirit led life not the soul led life emphasized.

God's divinely ordered marriage therefore must be based on both parties having their spirits quickened by a reconciliation to Jesus, and a deep intimacy with Him allowing the Holy Spirit (the teacher counselor, the spirit of Truth) to work through them in the marriage and lives. Self effort is out of the New Testament life, a life based upon the righteousness of God in Christ Jesus is that which pleases our God, the Father.

In John 20:22, (Amp)… "He breathed on them and said to them, receive the Holy Ghost". Note here too that Jesus breathed upon the disciples just as His Father God breathed into Adam. Our focus in our marriages should be based upon what the Holy Spirit desires. The breath of life or the Holy Spirit empowers the new covenant marriage couples, so whatever has no holy spirit has no life. God's spirit bearing witness with our spirit establishes in us the knowledge that we are righteous. Jesus came that we will be righteous in God through His finished work on the cross.

Our marriages should be based on the righteousness of God since we belong now to God's kingdom. Our marriages are to bear the fruits of the kingdom, the fruits of salvation which is righteousness, peace and joy in the Holy Ghost. Our marriages as kingdom people should yield the benefits of our salvation which is to reconcile men back to God. People should want to know Jesus through what they see in our marriages. This should be the prime focus of a new testament, new covenant marriage; for Christ came to reconcile man unto God, and we draw our life from Christ. (Ephesians 2:16, John 3:16. 2 Corinthians 5:15-19). God has given us the ministry of reconciliation through Christ by the Holy Ghost. God is love and so he gave us His only son, in our marriages therefore we should give the best of what we have received (Christ). By Word and in deeds we should show forth Christ and bring people through our marriages to him.

CHAPTER FOUR

God's Purpose And Plan For Putting Two Together In Marriage

When God puts two of his children together in a marriage, we must know that He is a purposeful God and therefore he must have a reason and plan.

As kingdom people, we should look to the Word of God to understand the Father's heart for such an act. We can infer from Genesis 17:1-7, 15,16,19,21 the first reason, why God will put two people together in the marriage institution. Here God put Abram whose name he later changed to be Abraham and Sarai whom he later changed her name to Sarah together. He gave them a common purpose to fulfill, they became one in purpose. Abraham was to become the Father of many nations, both of them were to bring forth the promise seed Isaac who is a type of Jesus Christ.

Fruitfulness in righteousness is the purpose for which God puts man and woman together in marriage. When Christ is made the Lord of our marriages, we surely will have our marriages pleasing God and we will be fruitful in Christ for God as we live our God ordained purposes.

In Genesis 18:11 – 14 (Amp)... The bible says" Now Abraham and Sarah were old, well advanced in years, it had ceased to be with Sarah as with (young) women. She was past the age of child bearing. Verse 12: Therefore Sarah laughed to herself saying, after I have become aged shall I have pleasure and delight, for my Lord (husband), being old also? Verse 13... And the Lord asked Abraham; why did Sarah laugh saying, Shall I really bear a child when I am old? Verse 14 ... Is anything too hard or too wonderful?"

In Genesis 18:11 – 14, We can see through Abraham and Sarah's marriage, a picture of God's thought pertaining to the new testament covenant as regards to being fruitful in our marriages as Kingdom people, In Verse 12, Sarah laughed because in the natural the situation she was facing was contrary to what she eaves dropped on as the Lord talked to Abraham promising them a child. It was a dead and impossible situation.

I believe God our Father allowed this impossible situation in the life of Abraham and Sarah for they themselves and us as new testament believers infact humanity, to realize that fruitfulness is not only in our marriages but in all areas of our lives can only come from Him our creator. Secondly, that being fruitful in the new covenant marriage does not need any fleshly, carnal effort. (I believe God allowed them to be old and be barren to show that only He God is fruitful and can cause fruitfulness in anyone's life. He is the source of fruitfulness in righteousness Abraham and Sarah were made righteous by God not because they were all good, but because they choose to believe in Him.

See Romans 4:2, 3 (Amp) "For if Abraham was justified, established as just by acquittal from guilt by good works (that he did, then) he has grounds for boasting. But not before God; Verse 3, For what does the scripture say? Abraham believed in (trusted) God, and it was credited to his account as righteousness (right living and right standing with God) (See also Genesis 15:6).

Abraham and Sarah therefore bore the fruit of righteousness that is their son Isaac. Fruitfulness will always be the fruit of the righteousness of Good under the new covenant, Isaac being a type of the fruit of righteousness.

Romans 7:4 also explicitly helps to express Father's heart as to our marriages under the new covenant bearing fruits of righteousness. The two subsequent verses (see 2,3) compares our relationship to Jesus under the new testament as like unto a couple the law and us being dead from the Law our then husband, and now being married to Christ. Now since we belong to another (Christ our Lord) God's plan is for us to bear fruit. This picture pertains to not only our personal lives, but also to our marriages under the New Testament covenant as his children.

By the new covenant our deadness to the law goes to say that Christ died for us, so our marriages would be established from the Spirit of God himself bringing forth fruits of righteousness unto Him. We cannot bring forth fruits of righteousness unto God if our marriages are not based upon God's word. Can we sincerely say as believers that our marriages are bearing the fruits of righteousness which the Father prescribes in his word as being peace and joy produced by the Holy Ghost, (see Romans 14:17), as well as the fruit of the Holy Spirit being forbearance, kindness, Love, goodness, faithfulness, gentleness, self control and righteousness? (Galatians 5:22,23)

The second purpose and plan for God bringing two of his children into the institution of marriage is to have our marriages reconcile many back to Him. People should see our marriages and desire to enter into this institution and should enter to please God in their marriages as well.

The reason is that through Christ we have been reconciled back to God (Romans 5:10,11) Our old understanding and way of life is now extinct, we are new creations, we ought to have the life of Christ expressed even in our marriages not only in aspects of our lives. There has come a newness of life which is from God as he reconciled us back to himself through Christ. (See 2 Corinthians 5:17,18)

Our heavenly Father gave us a ministry, a way of life, a mandate and that he made us reconciliators of the dying world to Him, He gave us like Jesus the ministry of reconciliation.

The second book of Corinthians Chapter 5 verse 18 and 19 reads (AMP) "But all things are from God who through Jesus Christ reconciled us to Himself (received us into favor, brought you into harmony with Himself) and gave to us the ministry of reconciliation (that by word and deed we might aim to bring others into harmony with Him.) Verse 19 It was God (personally present in Christ (reconciling and restoring the world to favor with Himself; not counting up and holding against men their trespasses but cancelling them, and committing to us the message of reconciliation (of the restoration to favor).

We are Christ's ambassadors, God is making his appeal through us even through our marriages as well to be examples of the righteousness of God, exhibit his divine nature and character that others may see our lives led in our marriages and come to be reconciled to their creator.

It is of no wonder that God always uses the marriage relationship as an analogy of our relationship to Jesus Christ in the new covenant as his bride the church. (See Ephesians 5:22-23)

CHAPTER FIVE

God's Order In Marriage

The essence of exhibiting God's order in marriage is that his intended blessings pertaining to the marriage institution will be enjoyed by us his children.

There are two things to consider as far as divine order in marriage is concerned. We have the ORDER OF AUTHORITY and the ORDER OF SERVICE. We can glean from various bible verses to confirm the above thought.

The Order of Authority, is that which pertains to the man or husband in any Christian marriage. The second order is the Order of Service or Submission which relates to that which the woman or wife operates under. We may agree here just this once with the world and say (ladies first) by talking about the order of service or the order of submission.

Submission to many women is an antagonizing word, however from our bible perspective, it is an expression of God's heart as to what he by his spirit can express through a wife if she will let Him ; so she will experience manifold blessings.

The Art of Submission is an act. As an English word in the bible, the Greek equivalent word is "hypotasso" defined as.

1. To arrange under, to subordinate
2. To subject, or to put under subjection
3. To subject one's self; to obey
4. To submit to ones control
5. To yield to ones admonition or advice
6. To obey, be subject
7. To yield to governance or authority
8. To subject to a condition
9. To yield oneself to the authority or will of another.
10. To permit oneself to be subjected to something
11. To defer or consent to abide by the opinion or authority of another.

The word "submission" was a Greek military term meaning" to arrange (troop divisions) in a military fashion under the command of a leader. In non military use, it was a voluntary attitude of giving in, cooperating, assuming responsibility, and carrying a burden.

According to Psalm 133, submission is a Spirit ; the act of submission can be manifested physically through the way one acts. In the above psalm, we can deduce that submission descends from heaven like the dew and with it comes a blessing which is life for evermore. You cannot totally and willingly submit to any ordained authority if you are not energized by the spirit of God (The Holy Spirit) It has to come down from heaven unto you, it will affect every area of the one who willingly will submits life.

Our heavenly father will have us his daughters submit to our husbands; this is his will for us. Romans 13:1 says "For there is no authority except from God and the authorities that exist are appointed by God" (AMP)

Colossians 3:18 also affirms the heart of our heavenly father and he says "Wives, submit to your husbands (subordinate and adapt yourselves to them) as is right and fitting and your proper duty in the Lord (AMP).

It must be noted by all as believing women that submission has to be a willing act. One must willingly acknowledge the benefits and the importance of yielding to another's authority or opinion without being coerced or forced.

The word of God says that we are members of one body mutually dependant on one another (Rom 12:5) also that we should be subject to one another out of reverence for Christ. (Eph. 5:21) Jesus Christ is the head of the Church as the husband is the head of the wife in marriage. Therefore as the body of Christ draws its nourishment from Christ her head, so must we the wives submit to our husbands so that as they draw nourishment from Christ, we are also nourished by our husbands in submitting to them. This premise can be arrived at as we consider the various definitions of the word "submission which explains in one word the Order of service. As women our life depends on the nourishment we obtain from our spiritual heads, Christ and our husbands. We must willingly submit to authority and of course to our own husbands to avoid destruction. Ephesians 5:21, 24 declares "Wives, be subject (be submissive and adapt yourselves) to your own husbands as (a service) to the Lord" 23. For the husband is the head of the wife as Christ is the Head of the Church, Himself the Savior of (His) body. Verse 24, As the Church is subject to Christ, so let wives also be subject in everything to their husbands.(Amp)

In submitting to God, we establish as women our acceptance in Christ Jesus. Submission is not by choice, but a must for every child of God, even submitting willingly to worldly ordinances of men. God requires that we submit even to the rules and regulations set by men for His sake. This proves that as children of God we are walking in obedience to his Word (1 Peter 2:13(Amp)... Be submissive to every human institution and authority for the sake of the Lord, whether it be to the emperor as supreme".)

The second reason also being that men will see how foolish it is to prove oneself to others. It is wise to submit to every ordained authority (1 Peter 2:15(Amp)... For it is God's will and intention that by doing right (your good and honest lives) should silence (muzzle, gag) the ignorant charges and ill informed criticisms of foolish persons.

As women who till today are mistreated and disdained by society, looked upon as second class citizens, treated merely as property, underdogs, mere bearers of children, it is very difficult if we should carnally consider the art and act of total and willful submission to men who normally are the perpetrators of atrocities towards most women. The wisdom of this world will suggest to us as Christian wives also not to submit totally to our husbands in this day and age. (Bear in mind that some Christian husbands treat their wives no better than unbelieving husbands.) Our heavenly father will however have us submit and show respect and treat all men honorably. (1 Peter 2:16,17,18) in every situation I believe especially the difficult ones.

Knowing who you are in Christ and knowing who Christ is in you goes a long way to help everyone including women to have a healthy self image and confidence not based on the carnal or sensual but confidence in Christ and in his word. As a woman, submitting to your husband does not demean who you are, accept your uniqueness in Christ, know you are beloved of Him, and clothed with His glory.

God our Heavenly Father expects every godly wife to walk in divine order in her marriage ; and this pleases him. As mentioned earlier, to submit to one's husband is as serving God through ones act of submission and this contributes to the harmony in the home and it is our divine duty to perform.

The divine knowledge and wisdom in Colossians 3:17-20 can also help us as godly women to walk in submission to our husbands in order to please God (Verse 17 "And whatever you do no matter what it is) in word or deed, do everything in the name of the Lord Jesus and in dependence upon His person, giving praise to God the Father through Him". (Amp.) The word is here admonishing every woman to do whatever in word or deed including submitting willingly to the husband as unto He our Lord and be thankful. In being thankful for our husbands is seen by our heavenly Father as being grateful for our husbands who are gifts from him to us.

Why will the Word equate our husbands to the Lord Jesus our Lord in the above verse? I believe our Heavenly Father wants us to honor our husbands and see how important they are to the Lord. He has given them a great responsibility to take care of us their wives, us his daughters. The least we can do to please God is to appreciate God through our act of submitting willingly, honoring, cherishing and reverencing our husbands, showing our appreciation to God by being obedient. It is however not supposed to be a master servant relationship but it is the recognition of the husband's leadership, wisdom and tenderness.

Carnally we may often be tempted as women to see the frailties and natural weakness of our husbands which may make it difficult to willingly submit to them. We ought to focus on the Holy Spirits help to see them as God will have us see them. In 1 Peter 2:11 if we do not get Holy Spirit help, we will become sensual, carnal as we yield to our sensual and evil desires to disrespect and dishonor our husbands because of what we naturally see is wrong with them.

As Christian wives, our husbands are our heads by divine ordination and divine appointment. Our conduct towards them must bring glory to God and win the world and others to Him. And as 1 Peter 2:12 says "Conduct yourselves properly (honorably, righteously among the gentiles so that although they may slander you as evil doers ; yet they may be witnessing your good deeds and glorify God."

The divine admonition in 1 Peter 2:13 and 14 is to submit to every human institution and authority for the sake of the Lord. How much more pleasing will it be to our Lord, when women submit to their husbands in their marriages? The verse 15 of the above chapter declares" For is God's will and intention that by doing right (your good and honest lives) should silence, muzzle, gag the ignorant charges and ill informed criticism of foolish persons.

Now at this point, a godly wife may ask this question as to how she can practically apply and live this word. Should she submit to the difficult good for nothing, wicked husband?

In 1 Peter 2:18b-23 (Amp), we see Christ our Lord's example to us. As he Christ our Lord in obedience to His Father willingly obeyed to die for our sins, so must the wife choose in obedience to Christ, to willingly submit to the husband.

Once a wife willingly chooses to submit to the husbands as unto the Lord, God will surely honor and reward such a wife, for it is an obedience in submission not unto any flesh, "… be submissive not only to those who are kind and considerate and reasonable but also to those who are surly, overbearing, unjust and crooked. Verse 19. For one is regarded favourably, (is approved, acceptable, and thank worthy) if as in the sight of God, he endures the pain of unjust suffering," verse 20 (After all) what kind of glory is there in it) if, when you do wrong and are punished for it, you take it patiently? But if you bear patiently with suffering (which results) when you do right and that is underserved, it is acceptable and pleasing to God. Verse 21 "For even to this were you called (it is inseparable from your vocation). For Christ also suffered for you, leaving you (His personal) example, so that you should follow in His footsteps. Verse 22 "He was guilty of no sin, neither was deceit (guile) ever found on His lips. Verse 23 "When He was reviled and insulted, He did not revile or offer insult in return ; (when) He made no threats (of vengeance) ; but He trusted (Himself) and everything to Him who judges fairly.

God's blueprint to wives is clearly stated in Ephesians 5:20-24 and 1 Peter 3:2. Submission pleases God, it affords wives wholeness in the totality of their well being. Reverence, notice, regard, praise, love, admire exceedingly, honor prefer, defer and esteem your husband. An insubordinate spirit is agitative and loud. Proverbs 14 : 1 "Every wise woman builds her house but, the foolish one tears it down with her own hands, and Proverbs 21:9 also says that "it is better to dwell in a corner of the housetop {on the flat oriental roof, exposed to all kinds of weather) than in a house shared with a nagging, quarrelsome, and faultfinding woman."

As far as God's system is concerned, know as a godly wife that you have died to self and your real life is hidden with Christ in God, set your mind on what is godly. As to be noted in Colossian 3: 2-3, (Amp) Set your mind on what is above (the higher things), not on the things that are on the earth.

As women, we can act whichever way we see fit however as Godly women and godly wives we must choose to willingly honor our heavenly Father in all our ways. 1 Peter 2 : 16 -18 (Amp) sums it all up as it reads "Live as free people, yet without employing your freedom as a pretext for wickedness ; but (live at all times) as servants of God. Verse 17 a : Show respect for all men (treat them honorably) Verse 18b. Be submissive not only to those who are kind and considerate and reasonable but also to those who are surly, overbearing, unjust and crooked). Paraphrased.

Showing reverence to God goes along submitting willingly to the authority figures God has set above us, in this context being our husbands.

Submitting and obeying not only the gentle and kind husbands but also to the unkind overbearing ones pleases the Lord. This is because, as you choose to willingly submit to your difficult husband you recognize that its only by the Holy Spirit's help and enabling power that you do all things including the above ; (see Phil 4:14)

God's grace is sufficient for us, therefore in all things we must choose to recline and rely on the help and strength of the Holy Spirit's enabling power. The simple fact is that as echoed in 1 Peter 2:19, (Amp) One is regarded favorably (is approved, acceptable and thankworthy) if as in the sight of God he/she endures the pain of unjust suffering."

It is indeed possible to willingly submit to a husband who is cruel as long as we as godly women ask for the Holy Spirit's help. We must see submitting unto our husbands especially the ones who unjustly mistreat us, as service unto the Lord. (Ephesians 5:22 Amp" Wives, be subject (be submissive and adapt yourselves) to your own husbands as (a service) to the Lord. I must however emphasis that this must not be applied to where there are different forms of abuses in the name of religion.

This is the divine order of God for us Christ Jesus' followers in our marriages. God has put the man and honors the man (husband as head of the wife as Christ is the Head of the Church, Himself the Savior of (His) body. As the church the body of Christ is subject to Christ in everything, so must wives be subject in everything to their husbands. (See Ephesians 5:22 and 23.

It is part of the divine identity of a godly wife to reverence God as she submits willingly to her husband. As a wife recognizes the headship of her husband, she is unconsciously gaining a great benefit of divine protection, preservation and favor from the Lord, Just as the body of Christ accepts the Lordship of Jesus Christ and is entitled to receive blessings automatically from the Lord.

The whole of heaven I believe will back such a woman because she is willingly submitting for the sake of Christ, in effect she is willingly humbling herself to a mere mortal, but to God she is honoring Him as she honors her husband. As Ephesians 5:33b says "Let the wife see that she respects and reverences her husband, that she notices him, regards him honors him, prefers him and loves and admires him exceedingly (Amp), 1 Peter 3 :21).

What Is The Order Of Authority?

God created all mankind, to totally depend on the Holy Spirit's help when born again and requires the Christian wife to totally submit unto her own husband as a service unto the Lord. I believe that the reason was to help wives to depend on Holy Spirit so they can please He God in their marriages. It is easier for women (who are more emotionally inclined) to express their affections than men. In order to totally depend on God in their marriages and not so much on their natural endowments, experiences, or carnal nature, He requires wives to walk willingly in submission. This is hard generally for women, therefore in Gods wisdom, wives need the help of the Holy Spirit to submit to the authority of their husbands as He requires.

Men as (husbands) have been created by God to understand and operate easily in authority. Men are the authority figures, heads of the family. I believe God again expresses his wisdom here so men will also totally depend on the Holy Spirits help to be Godly husbands and not on their own efforts. God by commanding men (husbands) to love as Christ loves the Church is a very high standard to achieve. I am not a male, but I know that operating by the emotions is not a strong suit for most men. Generally, women are good at expressing their emotions but I believe men need to seek all the divine help they can help to love their wives as Christ loved the Church. This I call the order of authority.

Loving As Christ Loves

In 1 Corinthians 11:1-8, God through His word has expressed what the order of authority is in the institution of marriage.

In Verse one, the Apostle Paul mentions that any marriage must be patterned according to the order that puts Christ first, that mirrors the character of Christ Jesus as regards to his relation with Paul and then with Christ and his heavenly Father. As far as God our Father would have us be, acknowledging and up lifting Christ Jesus should be preeminent in our marriages, we ought to recognize him as the center of the marriage and our lives. Christ is the one who holds the marriage together the husband having Christ as his head and the wife having the husband as her head (see 1 Corinthians 11:3 which says "But I want you to know and realize that Christ is the Head of every man, the head of woman is her husband and the Head of Christ is God.

The man as the husband must expose himself to the knowledge of Christ; he must allow Christ to be intimate with him. He must allow Christ to love him and must be secure in Christ's love for him. As husbands are secure in Christ's love for them and submit to his love, then can they love their wives as Christ loves his body (Church) for you cannot give out what you do not have. It is therefore very important and imperative that a godly husband (man) should have a very secure relationship with Jesus Christ, he being the ultimate in his life.

Much controversy has risen as many have tried to interpret scripture here in 1 Corinthians 11:4-10 (I believe that the Apostle Paul was not talking about a physical uncovering of the head by the man but was borrowing from the traditional culture and from the physical to express a spiritual truth pertaining to divine authority in marriage.

What I believe he was expressing here is that it is the responsibility of the man to uncover (meaning to expose, teach, point) the wife to his Head, who is Christ Jesus. The husband's responsibility is to expose his spiritual authority who is Christ to his wife. He is supposed to mirror Christ to the wife by the way he lives, by loving her, as Christ loves the Church his bride.

In Genesis 2:15,16, the Lord God put the man in the garden (Eden) which means (delight) to tend and keep it, then commanded him by giving him instructions as to what tree to eat from and what tree not to eat from in the garden. God allowed Adam to name the animals and all created things, God divinely set order, in the garden;

He put Adam in charge as the head, the husband. This is the law of first mention in the bible, for no one was put in charge of God's creation, no angel, not even God himself. I must point out here however that while the husband is the spiritual head of the household, he must remember that his wife is also a priest unto God (Revelations 1:6) in Christ Jesus. Rev 1:5-6 Amp) also suggests that she is therefore not subservient to him as a second class person in Christ Jesus. "And formed her into a kingdom (a royal race) priests to His God and Father – to Him be ….."

Ephesians 5:21 (Amp) also emphasizes this "Be subject to one or another out of reverence for Christ.

We can unfortunately deduce from the following the occurrences in the book of Genesis that Adam did not or perhaps fully communicate to his wife Eve what God expected from both of them he being the divine designated head.

We could perhaps say that he did not instruct, teach, explain or communicate the instructions given by God fully to Eve. Jesus Christ who is our example, also expresses the above idea to us his followers particularly to the husband in John 13:1-14. Jesus who we know by scripture is the bridegroom to the church his bride, stooped so low to do the most menial work in a household, that of a servant washing feet. Jesus took a towel went on his knees and washed the apostles feet. As a husband even though you are the spiritual head of the house and even though Jesus in the verse 14 admonishes us to wash one another's feet the husband is the one to set the example of being a servant leader.

The Apostle Paul also made mention of the importance of the husband being the divine authority and leader in the marriage expressing the agape love of Christ. In Ephesians 5:25 therefore the husband is to love the wife as Christ loves the Church his body his bride. Christ gave himself up totally for his bride the church and so must the husband express a selfless love and devotion towards his wife. This is the whole core of how any godly husband should be motivated in his marriage.

Husbands must have an intimate relationship continually in their lives with Christ. Christ should be allowed by men to be their spiritual heads, allow Christ to love them, so they can love their wives completely by giving themselves to them as Christ has done for his Church, his bride.

The 26th verse gives the reason why husbands should love their wives as Christ loves his bride (church) and sacrificed himself completely for her. As the husband lives and loves following Christ's example he is teaching the wife by example. He is literally living the word, living as Christ before her. In so doing the wife is sanctified, that is set apart, made special to God as she sees the husband living by the example of Christ. As the husband also takes time to teach the word of God to the wife, she is being washed by the word, for the word of God is the only tool that can transform one from within.

The Word of God is alive and powerful; it is sharper than the sharpest two edged sword cutting between soul and spirit, between joint and marrow. It exposes our inner most thoughts and desires (Heb 4:12 NLT) God requires that the husband be the initiator of teaching his wife the word the reason being that as stated in verse 27 of the same chapter that she might be presented to Christ as glorious splendor without spot or wrinkle as Christ will also present the Church his bride to Father God without spot or wrinkle being holy and faultless.

Christ loves his bride as he loves himself, so he gave his life for his bride, his church. The Christian husband ought to desire and do the same towards his wife for this God's divine order in marriage; he must love the wife as being in a sense his own body. As Christ did not hate his body, the church but loved her, nourishing, cherishing and carefully protecting her so must the husband his wife. Christ always sees the church his bride as himself with no fault, weakness or flaws and so must the Christian husband see the wife. Both husband and wife must remember here that both are part of Christ's body the Church and are portraying the very nature of Christ that is why a man shall leave his father and his mother and shall be joined to his wife and the two shall become one flesh. This is a mystery according to Paul because husband and wife coming together are presented as one, expressing Christ in nature and character. Succinctly put in verse 13a of Ephesians 5 says, Let each man without exception love his wife as being in a sense his very own self."

CHAPTER SIX

How To Maintain Divine Order In Marriage

It is important to note that the devil our adversary understands what order is. As evil as he is, there is order in his kingdom. The enemy therefore desires to set chaos and disorder in marriages and he does this by causing the breakdown of God's divine order to create misery. There will always be the tangible abiding presence of God in any marriage where God's divine order is adhered to.

The responsibility to maintain this divine order in the marriage does not fall only upon the husband as the head, but it is upon both spouses with the Holy Spirit's help.

Let us now consider these few points –:

1. The refusal or lack of knowledge by the husband to uncover Christ to the wife will lead to chaos and disorder and the vivid example is found in Genesis

2. (If Adam had uncovered and taught what he knew of God and what God expected to Eve, perhaps she would not have listened to the serpent. God expects the husband to walk in obedience then teach the wife.) Also in Ephesians 5:25-33, and 1 Peter 3:7 the husband is encouraged to serve his wife as Christ serves his church, by teaching his wife, the bible puts it as washing her by the water of the word. Husbands must continually uncover their head Christ to their wives.

2. Continually as the husband loves his wife with the agape love of Christ shed abroad in his heart and not being bitter against her, will produce order in the marriage. Husband, serve your wife with your love, harmonize with her and peace and tranquility will prevail.

3. Divine wisdom is offered for the husband to treat the wife as a weaker vessel in 1 Peter 3:7 (Amp) "In the same way, you married men should live considerately with (your wives) with an intelligent recognition (of the marriage relation) honoring the woman as (physically) the weaker but realizing that you are joint heirs of the grace of God's unmerited favor of life, in order that your prayers may not be hindered and cut off (otherwise you cannot pray effectively)" Husband you are to consider your wife as a co-partner; though you are the head. You are to think of her not as inferior to you in anyway

considering her physical frame. Most women have higher threshold of pain and stress and endurance, but that does not make her superior either. To allow for divine order in a marriage the husband despite he being the head of the wife as Christ is to the Church, is to see the wife as a co-heir of the grace of life, for in the spirit there is no male or female. A husband's prayer going unhindered because he chooses to honor his wife by walking in divine order will yield peace and tranquility.

4. The husband though the spiritual head in his marriage, must with God's help honor God by gracefully stepping in his position as the divinely appointed spiritual head and divine authority figure. Many marriages have a breakdown of this, for the men do not step into their roles as leaders. A breakdown in this order, leads to chaos and disorder in the marriage. This allows the spirit of Jezebel to often attach to the wives as they have to step into leadership roles because of weak willed and weak minded men. This often leads to the wife having the tendency to control, manipulate and intimidate the husband and in fact she is lured by the enemy to usurp authority in the marriage.(see Genesis 3:6)

5. As a wife, continually choose to submit to your husband as you submit to Christ. As your husband serves you by loving you as Christ loves the church

(his bride) harmonize with your husband as he gives you that love which is pure from God. Continually choose as a godly wife to submit willingly to your husband, not having your obedience dependant on the senses as to what you see, hear or feel, but submit to him as a service desired by the Lord from you.

As a wife, it is easy to break divine order in your marriage by exposing the weaknesses of your spouse to others. This allows for dishonor as Paul expressed in 1 Corinthians 11:6. Cover your head, your husband with prayer, and encouragement.

Unlike Ananias and Sapphira in Act s 5:11) a husband and wife must always be in agreement with God based upon his Word. It is very detrimental to a marriage relationship when husband and wife will be in agreement to choose to love or act contrary to God's word, this behavior surely will break divine order in a marriage. God never wanted marriage to be a hindrance and or a strain on his children's lives. Total dependence on the Holy Spirit will help to guide couples to live in the joy of serving and obeying God.

Having Faith, Hope and allowing the love of the Lord to manifest through a husband and wife, helps to maintain, build and establish the Christian marriage.

The Apostle Paul mentions the above three spirits as very pertinent for the body of Christ to abide.

As a husband, the spiritual head of your wife, it is your responsibility to help your wife grow in faith, love and hope in Christ Jesus. Both husband and wife must realize that the essence of one's marital life is to glorify the Lord with their marriage.

Living in hope is both husband and wife having continually a joyful and confident expectation of their eternal salvation. Living in faith is both spouses leaning their entire personality on God, on His power, His Love and person, believing Him to be who He says he is and knowing he can do what he says he can do.

Having the Love of God manifest in one's marriage and living in the Love of God, is to have a true, affection for God and man. It is the tangible growth of God's love for us and in us showing forth. Paul the Apostle explicitly expresses the importance of faith, Love and Hope for believers in 1 Thessalonians 5:8(AMP) "Let us be sober and put on the breastplate of faith, and love, and for a helmet the hope of salvation".

A lack of hope in Christ in a marriage by the spouses leads to a dependence on the carnal, a confidence in the flesh. It also leads to complacency in the things of God. Couples must live with eternity in view. Couples must be cognizance of the fact that they are sojourners in this life. Life here on earth is temporary. The number one assignment that every couple must consider is the fact that they are to allow the Holy Spirit to reveal the kingdom of Christ in them and to reconcile the dying world to Christ. Couples must let their minds be on things eternal and desire to please God in every area of their lives allowing Christ to live through them and they bearings fruit of righteousness.(ref Galatians 5:19-21).

CHAPTER SEVEN

Why The Disorder, Why The Breakup?

There are many reasons that many in the body of Christ can give as to why marriages are breaking up so rampantly in this age causing much disorder, emotional pain, trauma and hurt in the children, wives and husbands. Some of these reasons are as follows.

1. Many couples though believers do not prepare adequately for marriage, many do not make the divine manual (The Word of God) their foundation and guide and therefore have unrealistic views and expectations.

2. Individuals have poor foundations for identity and security before they commit to marriage. Christian couples as individuals must have the confidence of who they are in Christ. Couples must have their

confidence in what Jesus the word says about them. Having confidence and a healthy self worth in Christ goes a long way to help have a healthy marriage/ relationship with a spouse. Marriage cannot fix who one is but the Lord can use situations in the marriage to fix couples.

3. Individuals enter marriage with unresolved past family issues, like coming from dysfunctional families. Individuals also come into the marriage with emotional baggages.

4. Couples fail to understand stages in their individual development and how it affects their marital relationship. The normal stages of a maturing marriage are the (a) Romance stage- where both couples are enchanted with each other which I call the honeymoon stage. (b) The Reality stage – where the honeymoon and enchantment is over and reality of life's situations and reality about each other sets in. (c) Then comes the building stage where both couple have to decide with God's help to make the marriage work as they choose and give each other room to mature. If these stages are not understand and worked on by a couple, surely disorder and chaos sets in, which may lead to a break up.

5. Couples allow differences and hurts to add up between them rather than forgiving releasing and

maturing. Unforgiveness and hurts become cancers which kill any marriage.

6. There is often a low level of commitment and faithfulness.

   In Hebrews 13:4 (Amp.) "The bible gives us one major reason why disorder could set in, in any marriage. As mentioned earlier God has ordained the institution of marriage. This scripture says "Let marriage be held in honor, (esteemed, worthy, precious and of great price and especially dear) in all things. And thus let the marriage bed be undefiled (kept undishonored) This is usually lost when couples as seen in the above scripture, do not keep the marriage bed undefiled, or honorable as a result of sexual vice and adulterous living.

To defile means to make foul or to pollute or make dirty "Foul"- is to make unclean or to turn the original state of something into what it is not. to make unuseful for its purpose. Biblically in Hebrew the word "defilement is a verb "Konoo" It is in a sense related to a kind of ceremony to render it unholy or the word "Moluno" in Greek – Is another word to mean to smear something with mud or filth. From these words we can deduce that the act of any sexual sin, fornication, the Greek word "porno" or the reference to the word "Bed" in the above scripture, which is the word "Koite" in greek (the marriage, bed, or intercourse, defiles any marriage relationship and can destroy a marriage.

It is to be noted here that the word translated "bed" in this verse of scripture, is a singular word denoting a particular act. Here it stands for sexual intercourse, a co-habitation whether lawful or unlawful. God is saying here that when marriage couples do not honor the institution of marriage and hold it in high esteem and also dishonor each other by either or both not keeping their sexual relationship pure, the marriage is bound to break up. If both should practice adultery or fornication, they have defiled the sacred institution of marriage. Sex should be kept pure and handled according to its divine function, to procreate and to be enjoyed, to be kept sacred. This is God's order pertaining to sex in any marriage.

It is the desire of God that we live pure in our marriages. In 1 Thessalonians 4:3, 5,7 says "For it is the will of God that you should be consecrated (separated and set apart for pure and holy living) that you should abstain and shrink from all sexual vice. That each of you should know how to possess (control, marriage) his own body in consecration (purity, separated from things profane) and honor verse 5... Not to be used in the passion of lust just like the heathen who are ignorant of the true God and have no knowledge of His will. "Verse 7 "For God has not called us to impurity, but for consecration to dedicate ourselves to the most thorough purity."

Passion is a strong deep often uncontrollable feeling, which could be negative or positive. Lust is the eagerness to possess or a strong desire to possess something. It is alright to want ones wife or husband and to have passion for him or her alone, but it is wrong and divine order is broken when the passion is towards somebody else other than your spouse. 1 Corinthian 6:15-20 (Amp)... reads, (Do you not see and know that your bodies are members (bodily parts of Christ (the Messiah)? And therefore to take the parts of Christ and make (them) parts of a prostitute? Never! Never! Verse 16 -: Or do you not know and realize that when a man joins himself to a prostitute he becomes one body with her? The two, it is written, shall become one flesh. Verse 17 -: But the person who is united to The Lord becomes one spirit with him. Verse 18 -: Shun immorality and all sexual looseness (flee from impurity in thought, word or deed. Any other sin which a man commits is one outside the body, but he who commits sexual immorality sins against his own body. Verse 19 -: Do you not know that your body is the temple (the very sanctuary of the Holy Spirit who lives within you? Whom you have received (as a gift) from God? You are not your own. Verse 20-: You were bought with a price (purchased with a preciousness and paid for, made His own) so then, honor God and bring glory to Him in your body.

To make love to your husband or wife can be compared with when we get intimate with the Lord in communion as we eat his body and drink his blood (ref John 6). Now this is what I personally relate it with. As we are in a covenant relationship as believers with our Lord Jesus, so are we in covenant with our spouses. We are joined to him as the above scripture echoes. We belong as husband and wife to each other because of the covenant of marriage. This is the only time when the spirit, soul and the body of a couple intertwine and become one. This is the only time that I believe as a couple you re-enact the covenant you made before God on your day of marriage. So why do you join yourself through the act of sex (which I say the act of lovemaking) to someone you are not in covenant with? This act definitely goes to break the divine order in any marriage, chaos will automatically set in.

The word of God is indeed the believers manual for living in the order of God pertaining to every aspect of life. Many marriages are misaligned to the order of God because both husband and or wife deprive each other of their right to their bodies. In 1 Corinthians 7:3 (Amp.). The husband should give to his wife her conjugal rights (goodwill, kindness and what is due her as his wife), and likewise the wife to her husband. Verse 4 continues 'for the wife does not have (exclusive) authority and control over her own body, but the husband has: likewise the husband does not have (exclusive) authority and control over his body, but the wife (has her rights). Verse 5:- Do not refuse and deprive and defraud each other (of your due marital rights) except perhaps by mutual consent for a time, so that you may devote yourselves unhindered to prayer but afterwards, resume marital relations ; lest Satan tempt you (to sin) through your lack of restraint of sexual desire. Not giving yourself to each other when needed is pride because both spouses do not belong to themselves but to Christ, the Holy Spirit and to each other. The enemy who is the author of chaos, discord and confusion is given a foothold in marriages when independence and pride sets in.

CHAPTER EIGHT

Divine Order In Marriage- The Husbands Role

For the divine order of God to prevail in a marriage, some priorities must be set. The first and foremost priority is to be given by both husband and wife to God. Christ must be the center of the marriage, the reason given in Ecclesiastics 4:12. (Amp) And though a man might prevail against him who is alone, two will withstand him. A threefold cord is not quickly broken. When both parties have a personal relationship and intimacy with the Lord Jesus Christ it is most ideal.

As stated in Matthew 22:37-40, we can infer that a deep intimate relationship with Christ by both spouses affords support from the sovereign Christ for comfort in times of trouble, The Holy Spirit who is the believers comforter is mandated by God through the finished work of Christ to be one called alongside to help. Holy Spirit is the encourager, the Teacher, the one who will lead the believer into all the truth of God and his word. Direction, correction, instruction, godly wisdom and strength cannot be adequately experienced without plugging into the divine source who is Jesus Christ (see ref. John 14:26 (Amp)" But the Helper, Comforter, Advocate, Intercessor, Counselor, Strengthener, Standby, the Holy Spirit, whom the Father will send in my name, (in my place to represent me and act on my behalf), He will teach you all things. And He will help you remember everything that I have told you."

Secondly, the husband must take his place as divinely ordained to be the head of the marriage and the wife for divine order to prevail. (Ephesians 5:23, 1 Corinthians 11:3).

In some Christian marriages it is unfortunate that some men do not understand their God given roles as leaders, heads. Their understanding of being heads to them is to be vindictive, lord it over their wives and treat them as unimportant and insignificant, feeling superior to them. This behavior tends to undermine the self worth of the wife, or tends to cause her to be rebellious and stubborn.

Husbands should want divine order in their marriages looking unto the example of Jesus Christ and His body the Church. Husbands have to be servant leaders honoring, revering, respecting and cherishing their wives. Husbands must see their wives from God's perspective as gifts to be cherished and nurtured. No matter how rebellious and full of faults a wife is, she will answer to the love of her godly husband positively, for this perfect love being shown her will cover her sins (1 Peter 4:8) Proverbs 10:12.

The Godly love the man will show could be by confronting in grace any offenses; of course over looking and forgiving when necessary, but not being vindictive and overbearing.

Husbands should not forgo their responsibilities as nurtures, protectors, providers of love and understanding, financial supporters to their wives and children. It is to be noted here that divine order is for both husband and wife to see their heavenly Father as their source (this should be taught the children too) their jobs or professions are streams through which God will use to supply their family needs. This responsibility of providing should never be left for the wife to shoulder alone when the man can help. Lastly the Christian godly husband must provide romantic affection and security and be a Godly example. This will ensure divine order in marriage.

A godly husband must be content only with the godly romantic love of his wife (with help of the Holy Spirit) not breaking faith with the wife by seeking sensual pleasures with other women. Proverbs 5:18-23 helps us here "Let your wife be a fountain of blessing for you. Rejoice in the wife of your youth verse 19, she is a loving deer, graceful doe. Let her breasts satisfy you always. May you always be captivated by her love. Verse 20, Why be captivated my son, by an immoral woman, ... verse 21, For the Lord sees clearly what a man does, examining every path he takes verse 22 An evil man is held captive by his own sins, they are ropes that catch and hold him verse 23 He will die for lack of self control; he will be lost because of his great foolishness." NLT. He must be a husband of one wife (1 Tim 3:2) self control, gentle, considerate and free from the love of money.

The Wife's Role

To have divine order in marriage, it is very important for the Christian wife to know her role as not being superior to the husband but to know her role as the help meet.(The one called alongside to help. Though the help meet, she is very important in the marriage. The wife is to however know that it is not her place to usurp authority and be the leader in the home. This often happens when the wife earns more than the husband, or when the husband is not responsible as the leader in the marriage. She is to surround the husband with aid and assistance.

The divine role of a godly wife establishes divine order in marriage in that she is responsible in keeping the home, (Proverbs 31:15,22,27,31) She is also to trust, love and respect her husband (Proverbs 31:11 "The heart of her husband both safely trust in her...")

Above all roles, the godly wife must have a solid intimacy with her savior Jesus Christ. The promptings and leadings of the Holy Spirit in her life will cause her to be virtuous, industrious, kind, and hospitable, in fact portray the character of Christ in her home and marriage. (Proverbs 31: 10-31)

Divine order is surely to be established in a marriage when the wife also cherishes, honors, reveres, prefers, regards venerates, praise and lovingly admires his husband exceedingly. (Ephesians 5:33) Amp.

As husbands are often looked up to by most wives to provide for romantic affection in marriages, the wives ought to do the same so divine order will be established in a Christian marriage. Wives ought to walk in love esteeming and delighting in their husbands as Christ loved and gave himself up for humanity (Eph 5:2) Sexual vices and all impurity, filthiness, obscenity, indecency must not be allowed in any wives life as a consecrated person (Eph 5:3 and 4 ref Amp...)

Role Of Children And Family

The family unit is very important to God who divinely established marriage. As a result of this, I believe God honors a marriage that is under divine order. In 1 Tim 3:4-5 Amps." The husband must manage his own household well keeping his children under control with all dignity (keeping them respectful and well behaved.)

The husbands often leave the nurturing and the development of the spiritual life of the children to the wives, it must be a dual responsibility, but especially the husband, the father should teach and train the children in the fear of the Lord.

Role Of Ministry, Jobs, Friends

God has called every child of his be it a husband or wife into a form of ministry. Often times, as husbands and wives evolve, the tendency is to lead a lopsided life where sometimes their roles are swapped or distorted. It is very important to note that jobs, friends and extended family should not be allowed to take preeminence over the role of God, the husband, wife and children in marriages.

The lack of divine order definitely creates chaos in marriages. Husbands must not put their wives first before God in their lives or vice versa. Neither should both spouses put their children first before each other. Nor should husbands and wives put their jobs first before each other nor their children. The divine order goes like this -:

God
Husband
Wife
Children
Ministry & Others.

The Conclusion

Believers as non-believers must understand that marriage as well as the divine roles of being a husband or a wife is a ministry.

No one can be a godly wife or husband and operate in the divine order of God without the help of the Holy Spirit. There is much more involved in it than the selfish fulfillments for both parties.

A godly wife must desire to walk in divine order in her marriage. She must let her husband come home and rest. She must let her love be centered on giving, not taking from him; be there for her man. She must also ask for the help of the Holy Spirit to give her the oil of compassion and the sweet wind of sincere love to pour into her husband's work day wounds. Be there for your spouse.

1 Corinthians 7:33-34(Amp) "the Apostle Paul teaches that the married woman cannot afford to become so spiritually busy that she is unavailable for the ministry of marriage. The Greek word translated "careth" in the

above text is "merimano". This word means to be anxious about or have an intense concern." Thus Paul is saying "I want the married woman to be concerned about pleasing her husband and vice versa, even as you both please God.

Where should the mighty lay his head? Is your home a restful place, clean and inviting? If not Delilah, the strange woman's place is ready. She knows he is tired and needs rest and comfort first before solving any problems at home or elsewhere. "Delilah" says "come lay your head in my lap." (Men as divinely ordained by God, your wife is your best friend and confidant. Men, watch who you share your marital issues with).

Note that "Delilah" or the strange woman knows all men are little boys somewhere deep inside them. Every husband was a boy who started his life being talked to, cared for and taught by a woman – his mother. She will entice and manipulate that inner little boy in a grown man to control and dominate him.

A wife, who is aligned to the divine order of God in her marriage, will do her husband well all the days of her life. (The reference is Proverbs 31:10 ff). She will herself praise, honor and reverence and respect her husband. The husband will be praised by others and honored as they see the wives attitude towards him. The heart of her husband trusts in her confidently and relies on and believes in her securely.

The wife, who is under divine order in her marriage, will allow herself to be the extension of God's wisdom to her husband. She will know the right thing to say all the time. She will not be a contentious wife who will tear her own marriage down by creating chaos.

As a godly wife lives under the divine order of God in her marriage, her priority will be to maintain her home before her career or profession and ministerial pursuits. Seeking to please God in keeping his divine order in marriage as a wife, honors God, and affords success in other areas of one's life.

For the godly husband, the crux of walking and maintaining divine order in ones marriage is expressed in the thirteenth chapter of the first letter to the Corinthian Church by Apostle Paul. A wife will automatically respond to the Christ like love of the husband. Husband, chaos will not have its place in your marriage when you serve your spouse through the medium of Christ agape love. This is a great sacrifice but will surely afford divine order and tranquility. Do not be conceited or proud, rude or arrogant, be neither selfish nor undiscerning. Be not self seeking nor keep record of any wrong. Be neither unforgiving nor vindictive. Be neither unjust nor unrighteous towards your wife and children.

Be ever ready to believe the best of your wife, be ever truthful, and show confidence in your wife at all times. Endure everything under any circumstances in your marriage, and pay no attention to any suffered wrong. Express your feelings without accusations.

There are no marriages in heaven; marriage is of this world, therefore as Christians we cannot divorce from the things of this world." World is translated from the Greek word "cosmos" in 1 Corinthians 7:33-34. The Apostle Paul's use of the word here means there should be a concern for harmonious order in a married couple's home. "Cosmos" could mean an arrangement or order or a divinely arranged thing.

God gives the gift of marriage, but a husband and wife must do the decoration and walk in divine order to benefit from the wonder and bliss of marriage. Decorate your relationship as a couple, maintain and walk in God's divine order for marriage or the marriage will see much chaos. Choose to stay in your marriage and make it work with God's help. As a promise keeper, a man of covenant, love completely, love your wife passionately protect emotionally, lead spiritually, Protect the uniqueness of your wife as a woman, praise her publicly, be proud of her, see her as a gift, a treasure from God ; be sensitive to her.

All of the above if walked in and practiced echoes the Father's heartbeat – His divine order in marriage.

Marriage Prayer

God has joined us together in the covenant of marriage. We let no man, devil, or flesh, divide or separate us, for we are one flesh. We walk together in unity, agreement, love and faith. Living out this one flesh reality and forsaking all others, we cleave only to each other.

In the name of Jesus, we loose from us and our marriage, all strife, pride, anger, selfishness, offense, bitterness, unforgiveness, jealousy, resentment, defensiveness, and we bind us to love. We do not expose one another's weakness, but we cover one another in love.

It is not good for us to live alone, or in independence, so God has given us to each other as a spouse. We are the gift of God to each other, an expression of His grace for our lives, and we receive each other as such. By finding each other as a spouse we have found a good thing, and have obtained the favor of God. We rise up and call each other blessed.

Christ is our head. We cover one another with love, faith and prayer. We submit to each other willingly and with joy, and our marriage operates in God's order. We walk together and Jesus, the I AM, is in the midst of us. Whatever we ask in prayer we receive because we live in the harmony of agreement. We are a three stranded cord and we are not broken.

We love each other the way Christ loves the Church, and we give ourselves for each other. We love each other as our own body and cherish and nurture each other. We dwell with each other with understanding and honor. We are partakers together of the grace of life and our prayers are not hindered.

We let no corrupt communication proceed out of our mouths, especially towards each other, but only that which is good to edify, that it may minister grace to all who hear, especially each other. We speak words of love, faith and encouragement, and consider each other that we may provoke them unto love, and the good works which God has ordained for them to walk in. We take every thought captive to the obedience of Christ, and give no place to the accuser of the brethren.

We pray that our love would abound more and more in knowledge, and all discernment. We pray that the Father of the glory would give unto us the Spirit of wisdom and revelation in the knowledge of Him; that we would know the length, height, depth and width of Christ's love, and that we would be filled with all the fullness of God. We declare that we are clothed with glory and power, that whatever we do prospers; that God meets our every need and gives us the desires of our heart.

By courtesy of Lady Jeri & Greg Mauro.

THROUGH A LACK OF KNOWLEDGE, YOU MAY NOT BE FULFILLED IN YOUR MARRIAGE......

-Arm yourself with God's mindset!

-Experience God in your marriage.

-Confront the Enemy from a position of knowing God's order in your marriage.

-Is there so much chaos in your marriage?

-Do you wonder if God cares about your marriage?

-Do you desire to make your marriage work?

-Are you blaming yourself for your marriage being on the brink of failure?

If these and many more of the above questions are bothering you, then you need to know God's mind pertaining to the institution of marriage. He created marriage and He alone through his word knows how this operates. Only He has got the no-how in this manual, his word.

Printed in the United States
By Bookmasters